Light
in My World

Joanne Randolph

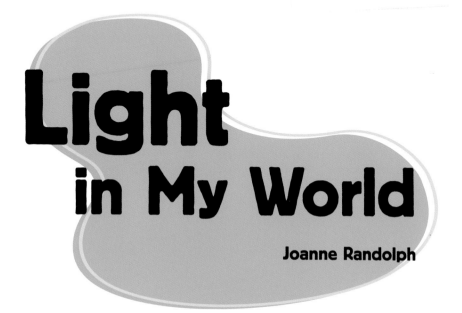

JOURNEYS®

Rosen
Classroom
New York

For Linda Lou and Lucas

Published in 2007 by The Rosen Publishing Group, Inc.
29 East 21st Street, New York, NY 10010

First Edition

Book Desgin: Julio Gil

Photo Credits: Cover (lightbulb) © Jana Leon/Getty Images; Cover (moon) © PhotoDisc; Cover (street light) © John and Lisa Merrill/Corbis; p. 5 © Darrell Gulin/Corbis; p. 7 © Jason Hetherington/Getty Images; pp. 9, 22 (rainbow) © Craig Aurness/Corbis; p. 11 © Ulrike Hammerich/Shutterstock; p. 13 © Norbert Schaefer/Corbis; p. 15 © W. Cody/Corbis; p. 17 © Firefly Productions/Corbis; pp. 19, 22 (fire) © George Shelley/Corbis; p. 21 © Andrew Cowin; Travel Ink/Corbis; pp. 22 (lightbulb), 22 (television) © Royalty-Free/Corbis.

ISBN: 978-1-4042-8420-3
6-pack ISBN: 978-1-4042-9194-2

Manufactured in the United States of America

Contents

1 What Is Light?   4

2 Light Everywhere   14

3 Words to Know   22

4 Books and Web Sites   23

5 Index   24

6 Word Count   24

7 Note   24

We see things that give off light every day in the world around us. Can you think of some of the things you know that give off light? Light is what makes it possible for us to see.

Light travels in straight lines until it hits something. Light can bounce off objects. Light bounces off mirrors. This sends the light in a new direction.

Light can be broken up by an object. Light is made up of many colors. Have you ever seen a rainbow? A rainbow happens when sunlight is broken into its different colors by the water drops in the clouds.

Objects that make light usually give off heat, too. Think about how the sunlight feels on your skin on a bright day. It is warmer when it is light out than it is at night, too.

Light can be taken in by an object. Things that are dark in color take in most of the light that hits them. The dark tar of a playground can become very hot on a sunny day.

The Sun is Earth's main source of light. Living things need sunlight to live. Plants make food using the light from the Sun. This helps them grow.

We use lightbulbs to give us light when it is dark outside. Lightbulbs need electricity to light up. Electricity gives power to many things we use every day, such as the television.

Fire is another way to light up dark places. When people camp they sometimes make a fire. The fire gives light. It also keeps people warm and can be used to cook food.

19

Light is an important part of our world. Can you think of reasons why light is important? Can you name some things that make light in this picture?

Words to Know

fire

lightbulb

rainbow

television

Here are more books to read about light in your world:
All About Light (Rookie Read-About Science)
by Lisa Trumbauer
Children's Press, 2004

Web Sites:
Due to the changing nature of Internet links, Journeys has developed an online list of Web sites related to the subject of this book. This site is updated regularly. Please use this link to access the list: www.powerkidslinks.com/mws/light/

Index

E
electricity, 16

L
lightbulbs, 16

P
plants, 14

T
television, 16

F
fire, 18

M
mirrors, 6

R
rainbow, 8

Word Count: 296

Note to Librarians, Teachers, and Parents

Journeys books are specially designed to help emergent and beginning readers and English language learners build their skills in reading for information. Sentences are short and simple, employing a basic vocabulary of sight words, simple vocabulary, and basic concepts, as well as new words that describe objects or processes that relate to the topic. Large type, clean design, and stunning photographs corresponding directly to the text all help children to decipher meaning. Features such as a contents page, picture glossary, and index introduce children to the basic elements of a book, which they will encounter in their future reading experiences.